KITTENS

By Grace Elora

Gareth Stevens
Publishing

Please visit our Web site, www.garethstevens.com. For a free color catalog of all our high-quality books, call toll free 1-800-542-2595 or fax 1-877-542-2596.

Library of Congress Cataloging-in-Publication Data

Elora, Grace.
  Kittens / Grace Elora.
       p. cm. — (Cute and cuddly—baby animals)
  ISBN 978-1-4339-4511-3 (library binding)
  ISBN 978-1-4339-4512-0 (pbk.)
  ISBN 978-1-4339-4513-7 (6-pack)
  1. Kittens—Juvenile literature. I. Title.
  SF445.7E46 2011
  636.8'07—dc22
                                                2010038501

First Edition

Published in 2011 by
Gareth Stevens Publishing
111 East 14th Street, Suite 349
New York, NY 10003

Copyright © 2011 Gareth Stevens Publishing

Editor: Therese Shea
Designer: Andrea Davison-Bartolotta

Photo credits: Cover, pp. 1, 3, 5, 7, 9, 11, 13, 17, 19, 23, 24 (all) Shutterstock.com; p. 15 iStockphoto.com; p. 21 Thinkstock.com.

Printed in the United States of America

CPSIA compliance information: Batch #CW11GS: For further information contact Gareth Stevens, New York, New York at 1-800-542-2595.

KITTENS

Kittens cannot see
at first.

The mother cat cleans
the kitten. She licks
its fur.

Then the kitten cleans its fur.

There are different kinds of cats. Siamese kittens have short hair.

Some kittens have long hair. Persian kittens have long hair.

13

Manx kittens have
no tails!

15

Kittens have 5 toes on their front feet. Kittens have 4 toes on their back feet.

Kittens have small noses. All kitten noses are different!

Kittens like to hide. They like boxes.

21

Kittens like to be up high. They like trees!

23

Words to Know

Persian kittens

Siamese kitten